DeltaScienceReaders™

Oceans

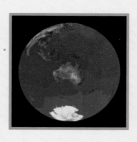

CONTENTS

Why Is Earth the Water Planet?

If you look at a picture of Earth taken from space, you will see that much of our planet looks blue. That is because so much of Earth is covered by water. Water covers nearly 75 percent of Earth's surface.

Salty **ocean** water covers about 71 percent of Earth's surface. Earth's four main oceans are the Pacific, the Atlantic, the Indian, and the Arctic. The Pacific Ocean is so big that all the land on Earth could fit into it easily. The Arctic Ocean is the smallest ocean. But it is still bigger than the United States. All of Earth's oceans are connected. Water can move from one ocean into another. Together the four oceans make up one big world ocean.

The word *sea* is used to describe a smaller part of an ocean. The Caribbean Sea is off the southeastern coast of the United States. This sea is part of the Atlantic Ocean.

Areas of an ocean or sea that are partly enclosed by land are called **gulfs** or **bays.** A gulf is bigger than a bay. The coast is often curved around a gulf or bay, forming a wide opening to the ocean or sea. The Gulf of Mexico is located between the United States and Central America. San Francisco Bay is between San Francisco and Oakland, California.

Earth's ocean is the only one known in our solar system. Water makes life on our planet possible.

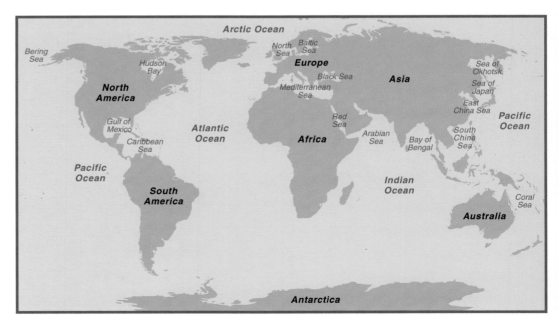

Ocean Water

Ocean water contains dissolved salts. One kilogram (about 2.2 pounds) of ocean water usually has about 35 grams (1.25 ounces) of salts. Most of this salt is sodium chloride, or common table salt.

Salinity is the measure of how salty water is. Salinity is usually measured in parts per thousand (ppt). This means how many parts of salts per thousand parts of water. In some areas ocean water is saltier than in others. Areas near the Mediterranean Sea are warm and dry. The water evaporates quickly. There is less water, but the same amount of salt. This causes the remaining water to have a high salinity. In other areas fresh water from rivers flows into the ocean. The water there has a lower salinity.

Water pressure is the force caused by the weight of water pushing down on the ocean floor. The deeper you go, the more water there is above you. So the water pressure increases with depth. About 10 meters (33 feet) below the ocean's surface, the pressure is about two times as great as the air pressure at sea level.

Density is the amount of matter in a given volume of something. The density of ocean water depends mostly on its temperature, salinity, and

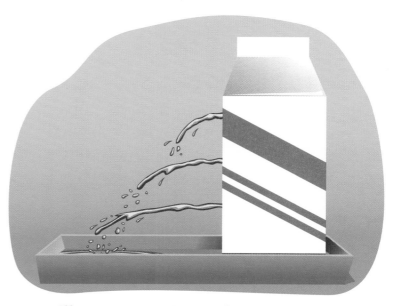

A milk carton experiment shows that water pressure increases with depth. Water shoots out farthest from the bottom hole because the pressure is greatest there.

pressure. Cold, salty water is denser than warm, less-salty water. A layer of dense water will sink below a layer of less-dense water. The top layer of ocean water is the least dense. The bottom layer is the most dense.

A hydrometer is a tool that can be used to measure the density of a liquid. The hydrometer will float higher in liquid with a higher density.

Features of the Ocean Floor

The edges of the continents slope away gently from the shore. The part of each continent that is under water is called the **continental shelf.** Continental shelf surrounds nearly all of Earth's land. The width of the continental shelf ranges from 10 kilometers (about 6 miles) to about 1,200 kilometers (about 745 miles). The average depth of the water where the continental shelf ends is about 135 meters (443 feet).

Where the continental shelf ends, the **continental slope** begins. The ocean bottom drops sharply here. When rivers empty into the ocean, the water flows along the continental shelf and down the continental slope. The water carries tiny bits of rock called sediments. These are dropped at the base of the continental slope. These sediments gather to form the large, gently sloping **continental rise.**

Beyond the continental rise is the deep **ocean basin.** The basin has hills, mountains, deep valleys, and flat areas. The flattest part of the ocean basin is called the **abyssal plain.**

Underwater volcanoes called **seamounts** are sometimes found in the deep ocean basin. Here melted rock oozes up from deep inside Earth. When

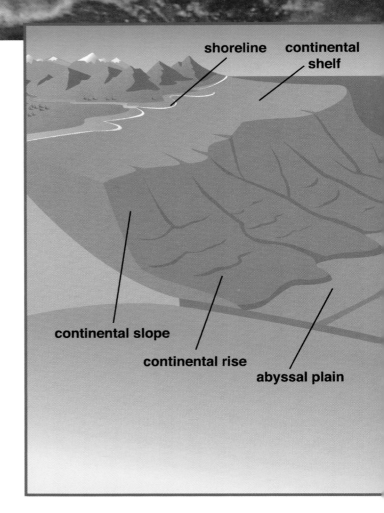

the rock cools, it hardens and builds up. Sometimes seamounts grow tall enough to rise up above the water. Then they form volcanic islands.

Corals are tiny ocean animals that live together in large groups. The hard cases they build around themselves form **coral reefs.** Coral reefs sometimes form around volcanic islands. When a volcano stops erupting, its peak wears away and starts to sink. But the coral reef keeps growing. Eventually, the volcano sinks beneath the ocean. A ring of coral islands called an **atoll** is sometimes left on the surface.

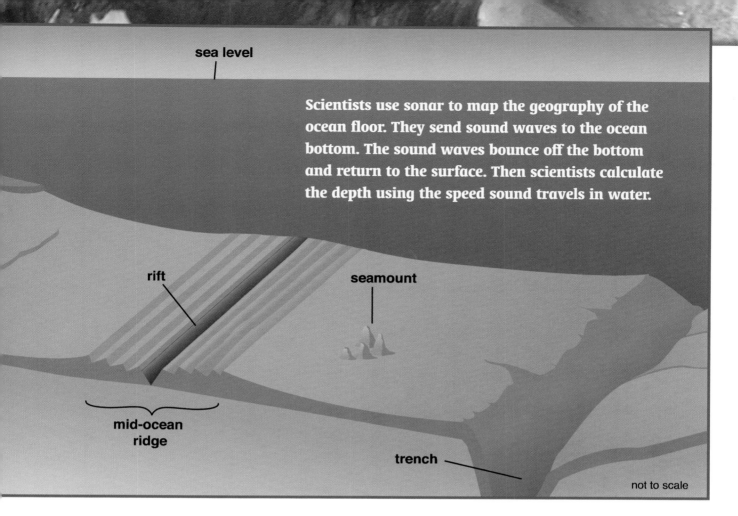

sea level

Scientists use sonar to map the geography of the ocean floor. They send sound waves to the ocean bottom. The sound waves bounce off the bottom and return to the surface. Then scientists calculate the depth using the speed sound travels in water.

rift

seamount

mid-ocean ridge

trench

not to scale

Earth's crust is made up of giant, moving sections called plates. There are about twelve large plates and many other smaller plates. **Mid-ocean ridges** are long chains of volcanic mountains on the ocean floor. At a mid-ocean ridge, plates are moving apart. This spreading forms a valley called a **rift** along the crest of the ridge. Here hot, melted rock from deep inside Earth pushes up between the plates. It hardens to form new ocean floor. This process is called **sea-floor spreading.** The ocean floor is growing about a centimeter wider each year along the Mid-Atlantic Ridge.

Trenches are very deep valleys in the bottom of the ocean. Trenches form where one plate is forced down under another. This can happen when a plate that carries ocean floor meets a plate that carries a continent. The heavier oceanic plate bends down and moves beneath the continental plate. This forms a deep underwater trench. The deepest trench is the Mariana Trench in the southern Pacific Ocean. The deepest place in the trench is about 10.9 kilometers (about 6.8 miles) below sea level.

Where Ocean Meets Land

The area where the ocean meets land is called the coast, or **shoreline.** Some shorelines are rocky. Others have sandy beaches. Waves and wind are always changing shorelines. When waves wear away, or erode, the land, a rocky shore is exposed. When the ocean deposits sand along gently sloping shores, a sandy beach is formed.

Many headlands are formed by waves that wear away softer rock. Cliffs of harder rock are left jutting out into the water.

Headlands are places where cliffs reach out into the ocean. Many headlands are formed when waves wear away soft rock. Hard rock cliffs are left jutting out into the water. Sometimes these cliffs are shaped like arches.

Sometimes people try to protect beaches from erosion by building jetties. **Jetties** are built of stones, concrete, or wood. They stick out into the water from the shore. They can help keep a beach from washing away. But while jetties may keep sand in one area, less sand may be deposited in another area along the coast.

The area where a river flows into the ocean is called an **estuary.** Estuaries have a mixture of fresh water and salt water. Crabs, clams, oysters, and shrimp live in estuaries. These places also serve as important nurseries for young fish and other sea animals.

This satellite picture shows the area near New York City. The estuary where the Hudson River meets the Atlantic Ocean is in the center.

How Does Ocean Water Move?

Waves

A **wave** is a rhythmic movement that carries energy through matter or space. All waves have the same main parts. The highest point of a wave is called the **crest.** The lowest point is called the **trough.**

The distance from the crest of one wave to the crest of the next is called the wavelength. The distance from the crest to the trough is called the wave height. Most ocean waves are less than 3 meters (about 10 feet) high. But during big storms, waves can rise as high as 30 meters (nearly 100 feet).

Most ocean waves are caused by winds that blow across the surface of the water. Friction between the wind and the water transfers the energy from the wind to the water. It is the energy in a wave that moves forward, not the water. Water molecules travel only in a circle as each wave passes. Then the water returns to about its original position.

A wave changes shape as it breaks against a shore. Water in the bottom of the wave slows down as it rubs against the ocean floor. Because the top of the wave is not slowed, it moves faster than the bottom. The wavelength decreases, and the wave height increases. Eventually, the top of the wave curls over on itself. When this happens, the wave is called a breaker.

From time to time, giant waves are caused by underwater earthquakes, volcanic eruptions, or landslides. These seismic sea waves, or *tsunamis,* can be more than 30 meters (98 feet) high when they reach a shore.

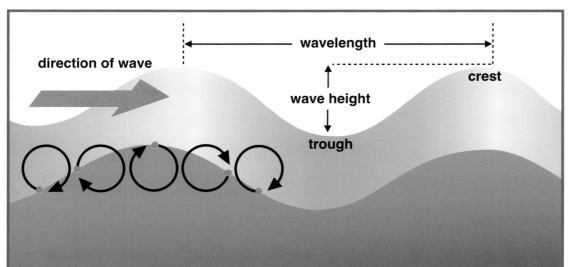

direction of wave

wavelength

wave height

crest

trough

In a wave, individual particles of water move only in circles as the energy passes through.

Currents

Currents are like rivers of water that move through the ocean. Some currents flow at the ocean's surface. Other currents flow in deep water. Currents can have different speeds, temperatures, and densities.

The force and direction of winds and the movement of Earth cause **surface currents.** Most surface currents flow in curved paths because of Earth's rotation on its axis. The Gulf Stream and the California Current are surface currents near the United States.

Differences in the density of water cause **deep-water currents.** These currents are sometimes called density currents. For example, cold, salty water north of Iceland sinks several kilometers deep. The water slowly flows south along the Atlantic Ocean floor. Warm, less salty surface water flows north to take the cold water's place.

Deep, cold currents rise to the surface along some western coastlines. This process is called **upwelling.** Strong winds push warm surface water away from the land. Cold, deep water rises up to replace the surface water. The deep water carries up nutrients, so areas with upwelling are often rich in sea life.

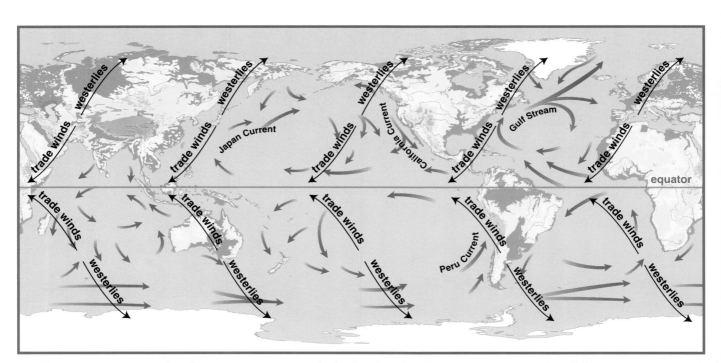

Surface currents north of the equator travel clockwise. Surface currents south of the equator travel counterclockwise. Trade winds blow toward the equator, while westerlies blow away from the equator. The red arrows show warm surface currents. The blue arrows show cool surface currents.

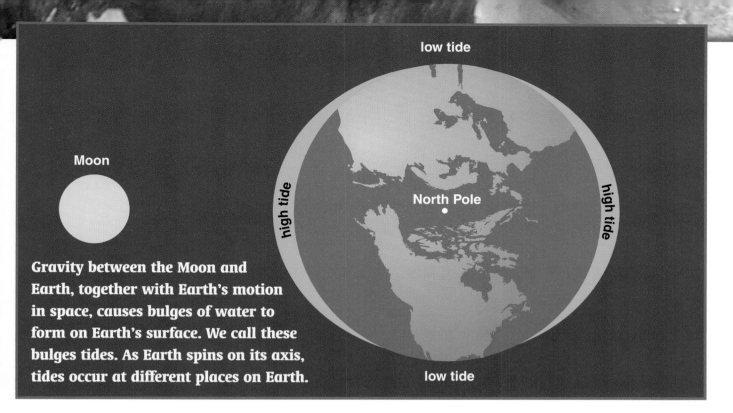

Gravity between the Moon and Earth, together with Earth's motion in space, causes bulges of water to form on Earth's surface. We call these bulges tides. As Earth spins on its axis, tides occur at different places on Earth.

Tides

During the day, the water level at the ocean's shore changes. This regular rise and fall of sea level is called the **tide.** When the sea level rises to its highest point, we have high tide. Later in the day, the sea level drops. This is low tide.

The difference between the height of sea level at high tide and the height of sea level at low tide is called the tidal range. In some places the tidal range can be more than 10 meters (about 33 feet).

Most places on Earth have two high tides and two low tides in 24 hours. Some places have only one high tide and one low tide in one day.

Tides occur because of the Moon's gravity and Earth's motion in space. The Moon's gravity pulls on Earth. This gravity pulls harder on particles closer to the Moon than on particles farther from the Moon. This causes a bulge of water to form on the side of Earth closest to the Moon. Another bulge forms on the opposite side of Earth. This second bulge forms because of forces caused by Earth's motion in space. These two bulges move as Earth turns on its axis and as the Moon travels around Earth. The high points of these bulges are high tides. Between these bulges are the low points that create low tides.

Gravitational attraction between the sun and Earth also affects tides. When the Moon, Earth, and sun are lined up together, high tides are higher than average. Low tides are also lower than average at these times.

How Do Oceans Affect Weather and Climate?

Earth's weather happens because of the **water cycle.** Energy from the sun warms the land and water on Earth. The oceans absorb and store much more of the sun's heat than the land. Some of the warm water evaporates, or changes to a gas called water vapor.

Water vapor rises into the atmosphere and cools. When water vapor cools, it condenses, or forms water droplets, around particles of dust in the air. These droplets form clouds. When droplets in clouds get big enough, they fall as rain or another form of precipitation. Precipitation that falls on land may seep into the ground. Some water is used by plants to make food. Plants give off unused water through their leaves. Some water runs into rivers, lakes, and the ocean. Then the cycle begins again.

Weather can change from day to day. Climate refers to the average weather conditions in an area over a long period of time. Currents affect climate because water warms or cools the air. For example, the Gulf Stream, a warm surface current, warms the air that flows over Great Britain and northern Europe.

Ocean currents affect the entire Earth's climate. Working together, ocean currents carry heat from Earth's equator to the poles.

The world's ocean currents act like a giant conveyor belt that moves heat around the planet. It can take a thousand years for water to move from the North Atlantic to the North Pacific.

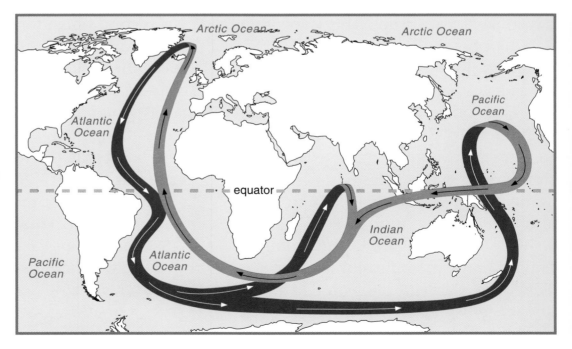

Ocean Resources

People have used the ocean to travel from one place to another for thousands of years. The ocean is also an important source of oxygen, food, medicines, water, energy, and minerals.

All animals, including humans, take in oxygen and give off carbon dioxide. Plant-like living things in the ocean called phytoplankton take in carbon dioxide and give off oxygen. About half of the world's oxygen comes from phytoplankton in the oceans.

Fish and some other foods that we eat come from the oceans. Some kinds of seaweed are eaten like lettuce. Seaweed also can be used in products such as salad dressings and fertilizers.

Some sea sponges are used to make medicines for treating asthma and cancer. Other kinds of sea life are being studied as possible sources of new medicines.

Many places on Earth do not have enough fresh water. Fresh water can be made from ocean water by a process called **desalination.** Ocean water is evaporated or filtered to separate the water from the salt. Then both the water and the salt can be used.

Many of our energy needs are met by the ocean. Almost 25 percent of our oil and natural gas comes from wells drilled

Irish moss seaweed is harvested and boiled to make carrageenan extract. Carrageenan is used to make products such as ice cream and toothpaste thick and smooth.

into the continental shelf. Generators powered by the energy from waves are an example of a renewable energy source that may be used in the future.

The ocean is a resource for many earth materials used in building and manufacturing. We get huge amounts of sand and gravel from the ocean bottom. We also use some of the minerals found in ocean water. Potassium is used to make fertilizers. Bromine is used in making film for cameras. Some minerals are found on the deep ocean floor in lumps called nodules. The nodules contain mostly manganese. Some nodules also contain copper, cobalt, and nickel.

Ocean Habitats

The ocean is home to a wide variety of living things, from sea turtles and sharks to kelp and killer whales. Most marine plants and animals have adapted to life in the ocean. Adaptations are body parts or behaviors that help organisms survive in their habitats.

Along shorelines is the **intertidal zone.** This area is covered with water at high tide, but it is exposed to air at low tide. The organisms that live in **tide pools** are adapted to live under harsh, changing conditions. Some plants and animals attach themselves to rocks. Other animals burrow in the sand. Crabs, clams, and snails are some of the animals that live in the intertidal zone.

Farther from shore, in the shallow water, is the **near-shore zone.** Kelp forests exist in some parts of this zone. Kelps are streamer-like seaweeds that grow along rocky shores. Fish such as kelp bass and garibaldi and other sea animals such as sea otters live in kelp forests. Sea urchins, sea stars, and sponges live on the rocky bottom.

Sea grasses grow on the sandy bottoms of bays and estuaries. Scallops, horseshoe crabs, snails, and small fishes live among the sea grasses. Tiny animals live on the blades of grass.

Many organisms that live in tide pools attach themselves to rocks. This keeps the plants and animals from getting washed away at high tide.

Sea otters live in the near-shore zone. When they want to rest, sea otters often anchor themselves by wrapping kelp strands around their bodies.

Many animals that live in the coral reef blend in with their surroundings.

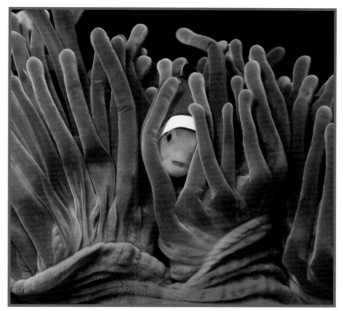

Sea anemones and clown fish often live together at the ocean bottom. The clown fish use the anemones as a place to hide and find food.

Coral reef ecosystems form in warm, clear, shallow ocean water. Reefs provide shelter for many animals, such as sponges, jellyfish, sea stars, turtles, and crabs. Many kinds of fish, such as clown fish and reef sharks, also live in coral reefs.

Even farther out from shore is the **open-ocean zone.** Tiny living things called **plankton** float in the upper layers of the water. Most plankton drift with the currents. Phytoplankton are plant-like plankton. They are able to make their own food. Algae and diatoms are kinds of phytoplankton. Animal plankton are called zooplankton. These include tiny one-celled organisms as well as very young fish, jellyfish, and crabs. Zooplankton eat phytoplankton.

Animals that swim, rather than drift in the currents, are called **nekton.** Fish, whales, turtles, shrimp, and squid are nekton. Animals that swim are able to search more areas to find food. Some, such as herring, swim to the surface to feed. Others stay in deeper water.

Many organisms live on the ocean bottom. Some, such as sponges, sea fans, and corals, are attached to the bottom. They cannot move around to find food. Sponges filter tiny particles of food from the water. Sea fans, corals, and anemones catch food as it swims by. Other animals burrow in the sand or mud. Clams and some mussels are burrowers. Sea stars crawl across the ocean floor. They feed on other bottom dwellers such as clams.

Marine Biologists

Scientists who study living things in oceans are called **marine biologists.** These scientists study marine organisms and how they interact with one another and their surroundings. Some marine biologists explore how to harvest food or medicines from the ocean. Other scientists monitor ways in which human activities might be changing marine life.

Sylvia Earle was born in New Jersey in 1935. As a child, she loved the ocean. Earle learned to deep-sea dive and studied marine biology in college. She earned a Ph.D. for her studies of ocean plants. She became the first woman to lead the National Oceanic and Atmospheric Administration (NOAA). Dr. Earle has set many diving records. She set the women's record for the deepest solo free dive, 1,000 meters (about 3,300 feet). She has spent more than six thousand hours underwater.

Sylvia Earle

Jacques-Yves Cousteau was one of the world's most famous undersea explorers. He was born in France in 1910. He helped invent the aqualung, also known as scuba. He also made films that let many people see ocean animals for the first time.

About Deep-Ocean Exploration

The deep ocean is one of the last places on Earth to be explored. The ocean has an average depth of 3,800 meters (about 12,500 feet). Deep below the surface, the water pressure is tremendous. It is very dark and cold. In order to study the deep ocean, people have developed **submersibles,** underwater vehicles. Submersibles are designed so that they are strong enough to hold up under extreme water pressure and temperature.

Some submersibles carry people. In 1960 the submersible *Trieste* carried a crew about 10,912 meters (about 35,800 feet) down into the Mariana Trench. This was the deepest dive ever! The submersible *Alvin* can go as deep as 4,500 meters (about 14,800 feet). In 1977 scientists using *Alvin* made a thrilling discovery. They found **hydrothermal vents,** hot-water springs, on the mid-ocean ridge. The

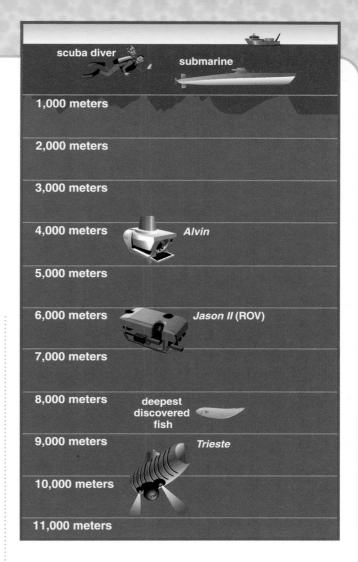

scuba diver submarine
1,000 meters
2,000 meters
3,000 meters
4,000 meters *Alvin*
5,000 meters
6,000 meters *Jason II* (ROV)
7,000 meters
8,000 meters deepest discovered fish
9,000 meters *Trieste*
10,000 meters
11,000 meters

mineral-rich hot water around a vent creates a habitat for living things.

Other submersibles are operated by remote controls. Remotely operated vehicles (ROVs) can be as small as a microwave oven or as large as a pickup truck. ROVs are attached to a ship above by a cable. Digital cameras aboard ROVs send images back to the surface. *Jason II* is an ROV that can go as deep as 6,500 meters (about 21,300 feet).

Glossary

abyssal plain large, flat area on the ocean floor

atoll ring-shaped island formed by coral reefs around an underwater volcano

bay small area of ocean that is partly enclosed by land

continental rise gentle rise at the base of the steeper continental slope

continental shelf gently sloping underwater edge of a continent

continental slope ocean floor from the edge of the continental shelf to the continental rise

coral reef ridge of coral near the surface of the ocean in warm, shallow water

crest highest point of a wave

current river of water that flows through the ocean

deep-water current ocean water that sinks and flows at deep levels because it is more dense than the water around it; also called *density current* or *convection current*

density amount of matter in a given volume of something

desalination process that removes salts from ocean water

estuary area where a river flows into the ocean

gulf large area of ocean that is partly enclosed by land

headland point of high land jutting out into water

hydrothermal vent hot-water spring on the ocean floor, usually on mid-ocean ridges

intertidal zone area along a shore that is covered with water at high tide and exposed to air at low tide

jetty structure built to stick out into the water from the shoreline

marine biologist scientist who studies living things in oceans

mid-ocean ridge underwater mountain range where sea-floor spreading happens

near-shore zone shallow part of the ocean that extends from the breaking waves to water 200 meters (656 feet) deep

nekton living things that are able to swim through ocean water to search for food

ocean large body of salty water

ocean basin deep part of the ocean beyond the continental rise

open-ocean zone part of the ocean that is 200 meters (656 feet) deep or greater

plankton tiny living things that drift with the ocean currents

rift valley that runs along the top of a mid-ocean ridge

salinity measure of how salty water is

sea-floor spreading formation of new ocean floor where plates move apart

seamount underwater volcano

shoreline area where the ocean meets land

submersible underwater vehicle

surface current current that flows at the ocean's surface

tide regular, alternating rise and fall of the ocean's surface level, caused mostly by the Moon's gravity

tide pool small pool of water left behind along a shoreline at low tide

trench deep, narrow valley in the ocean floor

trough lowest point of a wave

upwelling upward movement of deep water to the surface, especially along some shores

water cycle movement of water between Earth's land, air, and bodies of water

water pressure force caused by the weight of water pushing down on something

wave rhythmic movement that carries energy through matter or space